Unexpected Colors

Unexpected Colors

poems and songs by

Robert Moore

with illustrations by Dawn Marion

Beech River Books
Center Ossipee, New Hampshire

B R B

Beech River Books
P.O. Box 62, Center Ossipee, N.H. 03814
603-539-3537
www.beechriverbooks.com

LIBRARY OF CONGRESS CATALOGING-IN-PUBLICATION DATA

Moore, Robert, 1957 June 28–
Unexpected colors : poems and songs / by Robert Moore ;
   with illustrations by Dawn Marion.
     p. cm.
Summary: "Poems and songs inspired by nature and
   personal experience"--Provided by publisher.
ISBN-13: 978-0-9825214-1-0 (pbk. : alk. paper)
I. Title.
PS3613.O56665U64 2009
811'.6--dc22
              2009046411

Illustrations by Dawn Marion

Cover design by Ethan Marion

Printed in the United States of America

for Patricia Elizabeth,
my love and best friend

Acknowledgments

I wish to offer gratitude to my father, Robert Moore, for his constant encouragement and for his love of poetry, which has somehow manifested in me. I'd also like to offer thanks to Emiliano Martin, a good friend and a fine poet who lives in the Philadelphia region. He has shared some wonderful poems, many haikus, and like my father, shares a common love of music.

I want to extend thanks to mentors Stephen Scaer and Pat Parnell who have helped me look more critically at a poem's clarity and craft. I owe a debt of thanks to the Powow River Poets who have helped me understand poetry as an art form, especially Rhina Espaillat who is both an excellent poet, and a cheerleader for good poetry.

I would like to thank Dawn and Brad Marion for their willingness to take on this project: Dawn for her talented work sketching an image to compliment an idea, and Brad for his patience and care laying out the artwork and poems in the final product.

I would like to send out thanks to fellow poets and musicians who I've met along the way. I appreciate the connections we've made. Also, I'd like to give a big hug and kiss to my wife, Patricia, for her patience and support while I hid from time to time immersed in a space Pat Parnell calls "the creative process".

Some of the poems in this collection have been previously published in the following journals: "Silent Light" in *A Compass Rose*, "Anne" and "Tanager" in *The Lyric*, and "Niche" in *The 2008 Poet's Guide to New Hampshire*. Many poems in this collection first appeared in the quarterly, *The Poet's Touchstone*. My thanks go out to the Poetry Society of New Hampshire "for the furtherance of the cause of writing and reading poetry."

Contents

Poems

Beginnings   3

Long Ago   4

Departure   5

Only to Return   6

Ephemerals   8

Only Guessing   9

The Peach Orchard   11

Holes   13

Guidance   14

Trust   15

Doorman   16

Could Have Been   17

Dublin Road   19

A Change in the Weather   20

Reunion   21

Tanager   23

Anne   24

Wishbone   25

Waiting Room   26

The Musician's Dream   27

Oblivion   28

Crows   29

Mushroom   31

What to Do   33

Silent Light   34

Leaves   35

Les Oiseaux du Printemps   36

Light Sleeper   38

The Odds   39

Niche   41

Rites of Passage   42

False Alarm   43

Faith   44

Homes and Shells   46

Love   47

A Parable   48

Songs

This is Not a Protest Song   50

To See if I Can Do it Twice   52

The Evening News   54

Safe and Sound   56

Every Color of the Rainbow   58

Long Ride Home   59

If you want to do something,
keep doing it...

— Henry Thurlow

Poems

Beginnings

She gathers a ball of light
and cradles it in her arms.
Her eyes sparkle
with a mother's affection.
Her intuition tells her soon
the light will need more space,
so she conjures up a home
for its growth and preservation.

As her arms lift, they open
and allow the ball to fall
earthbound toward the blue,
embracing waters of the ocean.
Safe below the surface,
the light is left to propagate…

She looks on with an endless patience
contemplating her creation.

Long Ago

The universe was smaller than
the nucleus inside a cell,
at least that's where the scientists
believe the core of matter came.
And with a sudden bump in time,
the matter flew and everything
that held together or dispersed
was destined to receive a name.

And so the things that found a way
to use the light were labeled life.
And stars that lit up when the sky
grew dark took on the names of gods.
And things that could, they stood up on
the earth that was to nourish them.
They moved across the land by foot,
and learned to fly despite the odds.

The living things that would not stay,
they sensed the wear of weather more,
and when they could they'd reproduce
before the seasons changed their looks
to matter with still other names
and so divergent narratives
went on as if they had no end,
and these were written down in books.

Departure

The sky above is a clear blue.
I'm going to miss it.
I'm going to miss
hanging here with you.
I look across the field,
envy the needles on the pine—
their resilient green.
I wish there were stages
more abundant than there are,
something in between
attachment and letting go,
but for us it's all we know.
So if you go before me,
I'll watch the fall you take
and where you land.
I may not wind up where you are.
I hope you understand.

Only to Return

(translation on facing page)

Life is love—
it keeps going.
Attempt to snuff it out,
and it rebounds.
Try to rein it in,
and it sidesteps.
As it grows,
it carries enough room
for a bystander
to climb in
and get closer.

It doesn't define itself—
where it's going,
or where it's been.
In fact,
it's not going
anywhere.

Life is
love is
you are
so am I.

Solo Para Volver

(translation by Diane Arciniegas)

La vida es el amor, y se
mantiene llevando.
La tentativa para aspirarlo fuera,
y se propaga.
La prueba para reinar en él,
y para tomar pequeños pasos.
Cuando, se engrandece
lleva suficiente espacio,
su curiosidad
para subir y llegar mas cerca.

No puede definirse a sí mismo.
¿adónde va?
¿dónde ha estado?
de hecho,
no llega
a ninguna parte.

La vida es
el amor es
usted es
y yo tambien.

Ephemerals

When time runs short, does beauty fade
and occupy a different space?
When you attempt to tap into
your senses, does your hurried pace
to steer the wheel or ride the train
disable portions of your brain
to see beyond the rationale
that keeps you running in this race?

When time runs short, do colors make
a bee-line for a picture book?
Where do they go when tired eyes
ignore their energetic look?
They seem to re-emerge in front
of artists; or a common stunt—
to linger till they *can* be seen—
amused at how much time it took.

When time runs short, do thoughts have time
to germinate amid the noise?
The firestorm of busy minds
can leave a novel notion poised
to fall into the great abyss,
to vanish with a fated kiss.
Its saving grace—to hitch a ride
and surface in a youngster's voice.

Only Guessing

We pull up our roots,
climb into our cars,
and scatter…

Every day
along the roadside,
we drive by
an audience of trees.

If we could listen in,
could hear them,
could ask them why they just
stand there…

If we could ask them
if they'd like to trade places,
my guess is they'd grin
and whisper "No".

My guess is,
if the trees had their way,
if their branches were hands,
and we were asked
to root down one day
and stay home,

the thunder of applause
along empty roads

would be deafening.

The Peach Orchard

(A dream by Akira Kurosawa)

for Pat Parnell

Approach the orchard with caution,
for within it lies pure beauty.

It may lead you to think
you can bathe in its fragrance
and eat its fruit
and touch the flame
that fuels your mortal soul.

Be satisfied (if you can)
with the orchard's visual patterns,

of blossoms that unfold and grow,
detach and toss themselves into the hands
of soft winds; of designs in nature that throw
vivid colors and delicate perfumes in all directions.

Pay heed to the musicians and dancers
that celebrate the care of the trees.

Peaches, apples, almonds,
it's not really about the ripened fruit,
but the *growth* of the tree
its guarded limbs and roots that matter most.

Beauty is manifest
in the living things we see—
gifts granted by a hand we can not witness
but a hand that is working just the same.

To want more than this—
gentlemen, place your bets.
Strong desires are flirting somewhere
in this virtual garden of delight.
But strong desires are short-lived
and their final cost
leaves only the shadows of trees

and a heart filled with regret.

Holes

We're mostly space. But while a physicist
will study us and claim there's not much there,
it's clear on the surface atoms can be kissed.
Without much thought, we mingle, we lay bare
the notion that our bodies are felt, that space
outside our nuclei can sense the heat
that radiates from some internal place.
But if we ask if being feels complete,
well then, there's where the physicist and I
can look each other over and agree
the holes we cannot see are there. They're why
we seldom can be satisfied—why we
go looking for a fix as if there was
a liquid that could fill our holes with love.

Guidance

for Matt and Terrie

The wind shifts, rustling branches,
but no trouble for the kingdom.
The tops of trees bow and pray.
They sway with only the wind behind them.

Downriver, below the dam,
trees shiver when the wind is still.
The quiet river reassures.
It flows without fear of its own free will.

An acorn falls at its parent's feet.
A white owl spins his curious head.
He squirms as the acorn becomes a meal
for a chipmunk waiting to be fed.

The owl considers his own nutritional needs,
and now seems torn between three.
Shall he do unto the rodent
as the rodent has done to a would-be tree?

If he swallows them both, is it possible
that somehow he can pass
the germ of the acorn through two guts?
Would the germ stand a fighting chance?

In these woods below the dam,
trees shiver as the days unfold.
Owls ponder many questions,
and struggle with thoughts of growing old.

Above the dam the water rises.
Circles widen on the surface.
Clouds lift, the water clears,
trees sway and the river serves its purpose.

Trust

"...stick to thy foolish task,
add a line every hour,
and between whiles add a line."
    –R. W. Emerson

If life is nothing more than trust
in knowing we've been given time
to work on private artistry—
I guess instead of questioning
how long we have to hone a skill,
we might complete the task in parts
(and not to worry if the thing
we do will ever end). The arts

awaken when the mind has sent
an all clear signal to the heart,
restoring contact with a friend,
inviting wit to help cement
the work we left in pieces. So,

to raise concern about the end?
It's really not a key to who
we are. Our lives are better spent
when we can do the work we do
and finish what we started to.

Doorman

Doorman, take it slow,
when you come knocking at my door
I'll say hello. But I'm quite sure
I'm not the man you're looking for.

I'm aware the deal
you struck with me went down before
you gathered evidence to prove
I wasted time. I planned for more.

See, I heard this song.
I felt its warmth, and there were words
that drew me in. Now ever since,
I stare at setting suns and birds.

I still have to feed
the birds tomorrow, and I told
my wife I'd weed, you see I just
can't up and leave my chores on hold!

Doorman, take it slow,
when you come knocking at my door
I'll say hello. But I'm dead sure
I'm not the man you're looking for!

Could have been...

Uncertain of its origin—
it could have flown over on a broom for all I know,

its seeds tossed in the ocean,
then cycled in clouds to promote the rain and snow.

It could have been whispered in death,
when a victim was asked the reason for his demise,

or added to flavor a tea,
and after drinking a cup, inspired the soul to rise.

It could have been felt between partners,
when walking by a stream on an autumn day,

or flown on the back of a gull—
content to fly for miles above the bay.

It could have been hovering close
to the lips of a child, before she spoke a word.

It could have been something my father dreamed,
while lying next to him my mother stirred.

Uncertain of its origin—
I guess you could surmise it was a kind of feeling.

It may have explained the urgent need
for a prosperous man—to commence to stealing.

It may have been seen in a mother's eyes
while viewing her son's body on the cross.

It may have been felt in a lover's heart
when he finally came to recognize his loss.

Uncertain of its origin—
I guess it only grows and never tires.

It's been around as long as grass
was green, as long as seed was scorched by fire.

Dublin Road

When I was twelve, new houses looked like prize
hotels, and since their double stories could
accommodate a family of our size,
we chose to move in when the times were good.

It wasn't long before I found the dead
end woods more thrilling than our new address,
and so I followed where my footsteps led.
Other kids my age, some wise, some less

inclined to go to school, would rendezvous
in the clearing underneath the power lines.
We'd eat wild berries, ponder every new
invention, and pretend to drink cheap wines,

until our brains would overflow and we
declared that every one of us was mad.
One chance adventure left a kid and me
with bee stings running home. Another had

me filled with fantasies of gorgeous women
I had never kissed, or even witnessed
till I held one in a dream. Time and again,
I faced some neighbor's older kids who practiced

throwing verbal stones. And if and when
they came, I'd look away, I'd let them win—
unless they trashed my mother's name. Then,
I'd hunker down and let the games begin.

A Change in the Weather

It swept across my face—a whoosh of air—
and woke me as I pondered down the street.
The next one felt a bit more like a dare,
and stalled the forward progress of my feet.
I looked in nearby lots, at standing trees,
and saw their branches blowing in the same
direction; I imagined, seeing these,
my drive or lack of it was not to blame.

Long walks had always set my mind at ease,
but now a page of news went sailing by
the far side of the road. I could not squeeze
my eyes to read below the larger line
that warned "A Storm is Headed Up the Coast".
I thought it might be wise to turn around
when hail the size of golf balls fell. (I'd boast
at longer length of these.) And on the ground,

the weather now seemed more convincing than
the walk I meant to take before I ran.

Reunion

for Sarah and Jacob

She falls into another's arms,
the other holds her fast.
They do not think, they only love
to purge each other's past
with hands that know the gift of touch,
that sense a trembling heart,
with hands that soften muscles taut
with healing forms of art.

Their love can stay as long as they
give up their love—to hold
the time they have together with
contempt as they grow old.
There's freedom in the dreams they share,
there's freedom in their own
belief of where they'll be when they're
no longer flesh and bone.

Tanager

You come to settle but your stay
lasts no more than the time it takes
to wait. Your act begins each day
with fluttering wings. You trust it makes
a strong impression on your mate,
and hope her glances haven't found
another black-winged bird to date.
You perch a height above the ground
and, with your scarlet breast in view,
invite her to reciprocate.
Last year yours was her favorite hue.
This year it seems as if she's late
to look your way, and if it's true—
that someone else has caught her eye,
I guess there's nothing left to do
but lift your unfurled wings and fly.

Anne

She moves along the walk in daily grace.
Long strands of silver flow above her face.
Enduring lines extend across her skin—
they bear the past, confirm the shape she's in.
She may be humming music in her head,
or putting morning memories to bed.
She ambles by old buildings brick and stone.
They serve a kind of refuge of their own.
I can't say if she senses any dangers
from traffic rushing by, from passing strangers.
It seems she has invented in a day,
a way to cast her worries. Sure, you may
conclude "Her dreams are simple". So it seems.
I wonder if she thinks about your dreams.

Wishbone

What if two parties
were tugging bitterly
on opposite sides
of a wishbone,

and before the bone broke,
a large hand came down
and lifted the bone
upward,
into the clouds.

What would they do then?
Call it an act of God?
Shake hands?

What do two parties do
when they find themselves
with nothing to fight about?

Waiting Room

I'm in a kind of jam. I'd make
a move if she agreed to do the same.
She's counting the time between each ache,
and weighing in with dad about my name.
It seems like time stands still inside
these three dimensions, doing turns and flips,
and the walls keep closing in. I've tried
to nudge her but my left-hand elbow slips
along the lining leaving no
impression that she feels its inward thrust.
I pray an opening will grow
so I can wiggle through. But if I must,
I'll stand upon my head and let the force
of gravity proceed to take its course.

The Musician's Dream

He steps inside the station. He's intent
on busking as an unexpected guest.
He lays his case down, lifts his instrument,
and tucks it underneath his chin. He's dressed

in black jeans, wears a cap to hide his face.
He scans the room, the eyes, the shuffling feet.
Some passing glances slow, but few can place
the young man as they exit for the street.

He runs a bow across the strings and falls
into a dream. He listens to the sweet
notes rise. They soar inside the station walls
with all that make them beautiful, complete.

One youngster stops, is drawn in by the sound
of something his emotions understand,
but only seconds pass until he's found—
then hurried along by his mother's hand.

His music lasts some forty minutes long.
It carries to him heaven. He insists
his spirit lifts, and while he's gone, the song
is proof enough that such a place exists.

Oblivion

In the back of my mind
I know

that the wheels of war are spinning
in foreign countries,
that walls are being built,
that secret deals are being made
behind closed doors.
If my memory serves me,
I can recall
making one or two myself…

But right now
it's a sunny day,
and I need to hit this
little ball into a tiny hole
425 yards from here.

So,
if you would excuse me…

Crows

for Rick

You do the dirty work.
We do the final deed.
You supply the food, call it
a miscalculation.

You do the killing.
We do the removal.
And let me say our relatives
are grateful for the donation.

The only thing that's bugging me
is the *look* we get when you pass by.
The way I see it—we're doing you
a favor, so, can I ask why

you have a problem while we drag
our morning meal to the breakdown lane?
I can say with the utmost candor,
"Our furry friend is in no pain."

You can feel remorseful if
you wish to but I see no need.
Our work is disposing of corpses,
and their disposal is guaranteed.

Mushroom

Its cells multiply faster
than your mind can imagine,
its growth directed upward
in the matter of a day.

Its goal is not to seek
the entire world's attention,
but perhaps to catch the eye
of a traveler on her way.

To pursue a shorter route
requires redirection,
requires time to plan
and chart a separate course.

On one hand it's the mind
that works to save an hour,
but to view a thing unplanned
involves another resource.

Was the image you observed
a happenstance? By chance,
was it residing in your soul
before you ventured seeing?

Why do unexpected colors
seem to strike selected strings
of an instrument that vibrates
in the core of your being?

Is your mind the thing that leaps
when your eyes fall on a jewel
growing naturally on its own—
can your brain explain the wonder?

Is it possible the artwork
that thrives beneath the trees
has been living inside of you
long before your eyes looked under.

What to Do

Before our country's birth, the acting king
would hold clandestine meetings with a few
astrologers and thinkers. Their advice,
whatever it was worth, whatever new
ideas were heard, at last, they were his words
that silenced the oppressed when they would grieve.
He held a tight dominion over all,
and if they didn't like it, they could leave.

Today, we've earned autonomy. We claim
the will of one is one that journeys free—
that we were given rights that kings could not
amend—that our direction is to be
conducted by the spirit of ourselves—
that we, as citizens, were granted powers
that give each one of us the right to choose,
and so the liability is ours.

Silent Light

for Arthur Tufts

The wind softened then ended its need
to bend the branches of trees.
The songs of evening birds grew fainter,
then silent. A pack of coyotes lay
close to the ground—their heads raised in
quiet anticipation.

With the summer wind still, the night burst
into a swirling curtain of red lights and blues.
It was as if the looming atmosphere
held a mirror to the ocean—
and the motion of the sea
could be seen in the air.
The waves that rolled leapt left and forward
and eastward and northward—and the eyes
of the nocturnal creatures at rest
in the fields and the forests below,
glowed with the same hues
dancing over their heads.
Red lights and blues, then violets and greens—
and colors that artists might dream in a dream—
projected toward land and landed on scores
of faces that glimmered like miniature orbs.

For a moment, any pangs of hunger or fear
simply drained away.
For a moment, nighttime predators
felt as spellbound as their prey.

Then the wind went back to its bending
and the evening birds to their singing
and the coyotes returned to their stalking.
The night has its own way of talking.

Leaves

Leaves fall where they will when winter nears.
Should someone stop and ask them to undo
their need to fall, but wait a few more years—
I'd find out what a young man planned to gain,
if he wished every leaf to stay the same.

I'd need to know what made him cast a spell
to stop a living thing before it fell.
I'd question where his motive really came—
and doubt if it was triggered in his brain.

I'd wonder if his wishing was, in part,
inspired by a love within his heart—
a feeling that came once, and then it flew.

I felt a need like this, but then I knew
I couldn't stop a season if I wanted to.

Les Oiseaux du Printemps

for Joy Starr

(translation on facing page)

They come to rest and feed
and sing while eyeing a mate.

They come in yellows, in blues
with a mind to procreate.

Practitioners, all — of ritual —
any clues to reasons why

are beyond words, beyond thoughts,
better to wonder how they fly.

Los pájaros de la primavera

for Joy Starr

(translation by Emiliano Martin)

Se acercan a descansar y comer
y cantar mientras echan el ojo a una compañera.

Aparecen de amarillo, de azul
con idea en mente de procrear.

Practicantes, todos de—un ritual—
no hay razón alguna de por qué es así

eso está fuera de palabras, lejos del pensamiento,
mejor preguntarse como son capaces de volar.

Light Sleeper

You might think fireflies like us are only out at night.
It's true; at night we seem to have a common
aim, a simple message, "For now I will delight
any unassuming human I can summon."'

But bugs have other missions and work behind the scenes.
By day we fly from field to vacant pasture.
We land on bending grasses, cling to the dead and green—
noting harmful changes over last year.

We've scanned the eastern countryside, talked among the trees.
We've all agreed to spread an urgent word.
You may not think we're busy but we've learned a lot from bees,
and we won't rest until our voice is heard!

The news is not encouraging; we witness at day's end
the injured bodies lying in the street.
The road is always treacherous—roads designed by men—
our nervous neighbors simply can't compete.

Chassis' take their numbers, tires even more
will roll across the pavement with no fear.
Heavy-duty chrome-plated bumpers up the score,
and test the very mettle of a deer.

Our message after sundown is not a simple sign
to lure a youngster's eyes into the night.
We want grown men to understand our friends are in decline,
and we won't sleep until they see the light!

The Odds

Caterpillar crawls on land,
A hundred legs, and not one hand...
                    —David Olney

Journey-bound, she lifts one pair of legs,
then sets them down. They wait their scheduled turn
to lift a second time, and then a third
across the heated pavement, over lines
of yellow paint. She disregards a thought
to look both ways. She's over halfway there.
Her future looks in doubt but she has drive
and attitude to reach the other side.

Tall creatures stand in wonder. Others squirm.
They've seen the fate of woodchuck, moose, and deer.
They can't believe the pace with which she walks—
defying all the elements—a worm!

The luck she carries with her has no bounds.
Her first legs of a hundred reach the ledge.
She senses green, a change of scene, and though
new tufts of grass can house her, keep her safe,
I'd wager she likes living on the edge.

Niche

for Charles W. Pratt

Bend your head down toward the ground,
and find a stone they're clinging to.
You might be wondering why they're bound,
or how they keep their imprint small.

And yet, they're older than the trees—
the ones you often wander through.
It could be they're as old as these
old stones that used to be a wall.

They do it slow. They first adhere,
then multiply at maybe one
one thousandth of an inch per year.
(A year perhaps when growth is good.)

They thrive together as a pair.
And though their work is never done,
one hardly knows the other's there
and neither do the stones or wood.

Rites of Passage

One and then another,
women and men,
lift stones,
bind them with mortar,
build buildings, homes,
warm them with wood,
bathe, bear children,
sleep long hours,
dream...

Others
receive their right to receive,
enter through the opened gate,
immerse their minds,
learn a language, Latin, Greek,
study the need for resources,
bear witness to social pressures,
pose solutions to their peers,
to their government,
go off to work
for notable names...

Food is brought to their side.
Heat is pumped into their beds.
Keys are placed in their palms.
Buildings are built inside their heads...

A sign of the cross is gestured by some.
Where do rites of passage come from?

False Alarm

I'm sitting on the couch. I drop a spoon
by accident into an empty bowl.
Aroused, our pair of Papillons are soon
up on their feet. Their self-appointed role
as guards assumes I'm in some kind of harm.
They bolt across the floor before I shout
the sudden noise was just a false alarm.
And while they find themselves both looking out
the back porch sliding door expecting to spy
a prowler running off beyond our grounds,
they turn and stare at me implying I
can tell them why they bark at random sounds.

They know now it was me, but still they bark
to show me they're not frightened of the dark.

Faith

for David

No one's going to believe him.
No one ever does.

They'll ask him cookbook questions, like:
Do you have a pet dog?
Was it outside?
Was your wife at home? Did she see it?
Did you have the radio on?
Can you give us a detailed description?
Did it make a sound?

No one's going to believe him.

They'll gather up the information,
say "Thanks very much. Be sure
to phone us if you see it again."
Then, they'll hustle back to their
headquarters and file a report...
Newspapers will call him.
They'll ask him the same questions,
and he'll give them the same answers.

No one's going to believe him.

He doesn't want others to know him
by his last name,
so he only gives his first.
Says it was moving quite slow
for a ship that size.
With all its tonnage, he wonders
why it didn't drop from the sky.

And yes,
there were flames flaring
from underneath the craft, and yes,
it was silver in color with an aura
of red-orange, and yes,
it stretched to twice its size,
then vanished into thin air!

And no one's going to believe him.
No one ever does.

Homes and Shells

I can't explain this wish—to do—and then undo.
Can one assume dual roles, to bear the strain of two?

With one—to hone the art of self—to persevere—
and one—the urge to shed one's shell—to reappear

and live for once outside a cage—a selfless view.
Do skies outside one's self reveal a deeper blue?

I can't explain this need—to own—and then exchange.
When home feels more than spacious, I start acting strange.

I'm moved to scurry out the door with cash in hand,
and buy a bunch of stuff that sets me back a grand.

And buying with a warranty is never rash,
unless I need to turn the stuff back into cash.

I can't explain this need—to grasp—and then let go.
Philosophers find humor in our being so

committed to an object with a fleeting worth—
it fills a void till one can sense the turning earth

is made of things that come and go like homes and shells
and if we let them go, can we then see ourselves?

Love

I love to watch movies at two in the morning.
When restless, I find myself out on the couch.
Some people love chocolate, eat sweets between meals.
I'm one of those guilt-ridden snackers, I crouch
as sugar and caramel burst in my mouth.

When bored, I find puzzles can temper the wheels
that spin like an animal caged in my brain.
I look for the paper on Tuesdays; the page
with crosswords and horoscopes helps to contain
my two-fold desire for love without pain.

A Parable

after "The Star Thrower"
by Loren Eiseley

To set his mind at rest, an elderly man
took morning walks along a sandy beach.
One morning in the mist, he thought he saw
a young boy tossing stones into the sea,
at least they looked liked stones until his view
informed him they were starfish and the sand
had thousands lying there—the aftermath
of some big storm that left them out of reach—
unable to be pulled back with the tide.
The man as he approached could see the task
the boy had taken on. He looked again
at countless numbers lying there and thought—
no way could one boy save the life of all
those starfish, and felt moved to tell the boy.
"You can't expect to save each starfish son.
There's more than you could ever hope to throw
back in the sea. You might as well just stop
and let them be." But undeterred the boy
reached down, and then prepared to throw one more.

"They may not all survive—I suppose that's true—
but this one will." And he watched it as it flew.

Songs

This is Not a Protest Song

This is not a protest song,
I don't know what the fuss is all about.
We marched into a country. So,
we have some wrinkles left to iron out.

We don't believe in terror, that's
a fact, so what's the big deal if we treat
the folks that we don't trust a little
rougher if it keeps 'em off the street.

This is not a protest song,
we know the men elected have a lot
of choices there to manage every
day—they're forced to spend more than they've got.

And hey, no need to worry 'cause
we only need to send official word
to stampers at the mint; there's more
to print—I heard it from a little bird.

This is not a protest song,
we know our country stands for dignity.
And hey, attacks can happen so
we've tightened up our home security.

The guys decided we were best
prepared if marshalls rode on planes and trains.
But how you gonna stop an ocean
water spawning nasty hurricanes?

This is not a protest song,
we know the men elected are sublime.
They know the average Joe—I'm sure
they'd stop and help us if they had the time.

This country is the greatest place—
you get an honest feeling you belong,
as long as you don't kick up too much dust
and sing a useless protest song.

To See if I Can Do it Twice

I wonder what it might be like
to be a frog on a rainy night,
to wander from a dark lagoon,
to risk my neck beneath the moon.

I'm drawn and I don't even know
why the surface of the road
urges me to cross when I'd
feel much safer on this side.

But for reasons not unknown
I hop beyond the safety zone,
to get a better picture why
my buddies cross and croak and die.

I figure I'm the wiser frog,
if I stay below the fog,
dodgin' those that pose a threat
unto themselves—then I'll bet,

they won't see my shiny skin
or my green face when I grin.
I'll be on the other side
as quick as you can eat a fly.

Seems so easy first time through
when good fortune follows you,
but always this same urge to then
turn and then return again.

To see if I can do it twice—
this is my condemning vice.
Never satisfied but hence
to leave it to experience.

I'm older and not quite as clever
as I felt when I never
stopped to look or worry why
my buddies croaked before they died.

They were headed back across,
some looked dazed, some looked lost,
and some I think had stopped to see
what the hell was bugging me.

As I tried to hop and swerve,
I felt a pin go through a nerve.
Then I wound up on the curb—
I guess I got what I deserved.

I should've learned before I leapt.
"Look both ways before you step
onto roads that threaten twice—
take some morbid frog advice."

The Evening News

Wearin' the same old clothes,
wearin' the same old smile,
don't you know it gets wicked old
runnin' the same old mile.

Hearin' the same old stories,
same old exposé,
so much talk around the block,
can't help hearin' what they say

about you.
They say it's all true.
And what gets me hoppin' mad
is I begin to believe it too,
and I know everybody's sorry,
we all sing the blues,
especially when your pretty face
is pictured on — the evening news.

Microphones and cameras,
pens behind the ear —
you say you tried to smoke it once
but now you just drink beer.

And while we're on the subject,
can you share your thoughts
on our troubled youth today —
it seems they're tangled up in knots.

It's true.
They say it's all true.
And what gets me hoppin' mad
is I begin to believe it too,
and I know everybody's sorry,
we all sing the blues,

especially when your pretty face
is featured on—the evening news.

Get inside his head,
that's the bottom line—
and while we're all inside his head
let's see what we can find.

Catch them both in bed,
catch them in the act,
and juice it up just in case
we can't get all the facts.

Well, I thought about it once,
I thought about it twice,
the news is just a poor excuse
to broadcast every vice.

Does he sleep with her?
Does she sleep with him?
Did Mr. B. in privacy
live beyond his wildest dreams?

It's true.
They say it's all true.
And what gets me hoppin' mad
is I begin to believe it too,
and I know everybody's sorry,
we all sing the blues,
especially when your pretty face
is pictured on—the evening…
can't help myself believing…
every time I watch the evening news.

Safe and Sound

In this old town, we don't have metermaids.
We have cops taggin' tires,
and that's how they get paid.
They spend their time, when they're on the beat,
markin' cars and movin' "punks"
that hang out on the street.

In this old town, we don't have much crime.
We have petty thieves and kids that leave
their homes too many times.
And now and then, a scandal breaks.
Well, you might have thought an earthquake hit
with the rumble that it makes.

But don't you know you're safe,
don't you know you're sound.
Once you're safe, chances are
you'll stay in this old town.
It hasn't failed us yet,
It hasn't let us down…
Everyone still has a lot of faith —
in this old town.

On the western end, lies a dead-end road.
The bridge was shut down years ago,
and stopped the outbound flow —
and the fishermen, they don't speculate —
but ever since the road's been out
they say the fishing's great.

On the old town roof, we don't have a clock.
We have a slender lady there
that manages the block.
She stands aloof, and she works without a net,
and her balance must work well
because she hasn't fallen yet.

But don't you know you're safe,
don't you know you're sound.
Once you're safe, chances are
you'll sleep in this old town.
It hasn't failed us yet,
It hasn't let us down...
Everyone still has a lot of faith
in this old town.
Everyone still has a lot of faith
in this old town.
Everyone still has a lot of faith...

Every Color of the Rainbow

Cold winters have come and gone,
and the snow's been white all winter long.
I had a dream the other night,
the snow turned pink instead of white.

Well, white is nice and white is fine,
but why not green or grape or wine?
Wouldn't it be nice to see it snow
every color of the rainbow.

It may be hard to see the hues
when the snow comes fallin' down.
But when the sun comes shinin' through,
they'll be a rainbow of colors
in every town.

When the snow begins to fall
all the kids will have a ball—
jumpin' and a thumpin' in the snowy towns
covered in blues and reds and browns.

I've got a wish for Santa next year,
a wish that I hope he can hear.
Bring us a gift that we can share
with the whole world everywhere.

It may be hard to see the hues
when the snow comes fallin' down.
But when the sun comes shinin' through,
they'll be a rainbow of colors in every town.

When the winter winds begin to blow,
let the colors begin to show.
Wouldn't it be nice to see it snow
every color of the rainbow.

Long Ride Home

Rode by this barroom one too many times.
Couldn't see the harm done, couldn't see the crime.
Been on the wagon, off and on for years.
Learned to do the backstroke in my own beers.

I think it was a Wednesday, yes I guess it was.
Thought I needed counseling, or was it just a buzz?
Wound up on the sidewalk, 'neath the stars above.
Heard a choir of angels singing songs of love.

"Boy, you're lookin' tired now, come and stay with us.
You won't need a wagon where you're goin'.
Come and step inside our solar-driven bus
with trumpets and saxophones a-blowin'."

Figured I was dreamin'. Figured I was high.
Ridin' with a busload of angels in the sky.
Picked a few more winos up along the way.
Started lookin' more and more like judgment day.

We pulled up to the gate, and we all said hello.
Hopin' that the entrance did not lead below.
An angel in a bathrobe handed me a key.
She said turn it gently and get up off your knee.

"Boy, you're lookin' tired now, come and stay inside.
You won't need a wagon when you're through.
We'll show you how you lived, and we'll show you how you died,
and we'll teach you how to play a song or two."

Woke up in the jailhouse later the next day.
The guard said my condition was tough now to explain.
Wasn't sure if I was half alive or dead.
Told me "Hallelujah" was the last word I said.

Well, now I'm high and dry and I guess I've been forgiven
for my drunken days and my thoughtless ways of livin'.
Learnin' how to play a trumpet in the band
just in case an angel takes me by the hand.

"Boy, you're lookin' tired now, come and stay with us.
You won't need a wagon where you're goin'.
It's easier to see the sunshine from the dust
when the light within your eyes is a-growin'."

About the author

Robert Moore has been writing poetry since the early 1990s. He self-published an earlier collection of poems, *A Bridge with a View* (1997, Little Rabbit Press). He is the editor of a literary journal, *The Lit Fuse,* a collection of poems, stories, and artwork for the First Unitarian Universalist Society of Exeter in Exeter, New Hampshire. He has had poems published in several literary journals, including *The Lyric, Compass Rose,* and *The Poet's Touchstone.*

Moore is a composer of songs and guitar instrumentals and performs as a guitarist and singer for the acoustic-driven group "Sylvan Roots." He is a current member of the Hyla Brook Poets, the Seacoast Writers Association, the Poetry Society of New Hampshire, and the Powow River Poets. Since 1999, his day job is as a science teacher at Pelham High School in Pelham, New Hampshire.